THE GEN Z LEXICON

A Clear Guide to Understanding and Using Modern Slang

Master Modern Expressions, Strengthen Connections, and Improve Communication

Janet E. Shaw

Copyright © 2024 by Janet E. Shaw.

Disclaimer:

The advice and strategies contained herein may only be suitable for some situations. This work is sold with the understanding that the author and publisher are not engaged in rendering professional services. If professional assistance is required, the services of a competent professional should be sought. The author and publisher specifically disclaim any liability incurred from the use or application of the contents of this book.

Table of Contents

Introduction..5

Chapter 1... 10

The Rise of Gen Z Slang.. 10

Historical Context.. 11

The Role of TikTok... 13

Key Influences on Gen Z Slang............................ 16

Chapter 2... 22

Breaking Down Common Gen Z Slang Terms.................. 22

The Essential Vocabulary.................................... 22

Examples to Include... 29

Chapter 3... 36

How to Use Gen Z Slang Effectively........................ 36

Using Slang in Conversation................................ 36

Slang in Professional Settings.............................41

Overcoming the Fear of Sounding "Old"................47

Chapter 4... 54

Slang to Avoid or Use Sparingly............................ 54

Slang That's Gone Too Far..................................54

When to Let Slang Die...58

Chapter 5... 66

The Future of Gen Z Slang.................................... 66

The Evolution of Slang..66

What's Next?... 68

The Role of Technology...................................... 71

Chapter 6... 78

Understanding the Cultural Significance of Slang...........78

Slang as Cultural Expression............................78

Slang and Identity..80

The Global Spread of Slang........................... 83

Chapter 7...**88**

Building Stronger Relationships Through Language......88

Communication Across Generations....................... 88

The Role of Slang in Strengthening Personal
Relationships.. 90

When to Use Slang and When to Be Formal...........94

Conclusion.. **100**

Recap of Key Points....................................... 100

Final Thoughts on Slang.................................102

Appendices.. **106**

Appendix A: Slang Cheat Sheet........................... 106

Appendix B: Resources for Learning More............. 111

About the Author... **116**

Introduction

Imagine walking into a room full of people. You're there for a meeting, a family gathering, or even just hanging out with friends. The atmosphere is buzzing with energy. But something's off. Everyone seems to be speaking a different language, one that's fast, punchy, and unfamiliar. You're not quite sure if they're joking, complimenting each other, or just talking nonsense. Words like "Bet", "Cap", and "Vibe" float through the air like a secret code that you're not part of.

You nod along, hoping no one notices your confusion. But deep down, you're thinking: What is going on here?

Welcome to the world of Gen Z—a generation that communicates not just with words, but with an entire lexicon that feels like a foreign language to anyone outside their social circle. Born roughly between 1997 and 2012, Gen Z has created a dynamic, fast-paced, and endlessly evolving slang culture. From TikTok to Snapchat, Instagram to Twitter, their language has spread like wildfire, leaving many older generations in the dust. And here's the kicker: this is the language of the future.

So why does this matter to you?

Because in today's world, communication isn't just about sharing information—it's about connection. Whether you're in a professional setting, a casual conversation with friends, or trying to bond with a younger family member, understanding the language of Gen Z is the key to unlocking stronger relationships. It's about breaking down barriers and showing that you're in tune with the times. Without it, you risk becoming disconnected, missing out on opportunities to truly engage with the world around you.

But don't worry. That's where this book comes in.

This is not just a dictionary of slang. It's a bridge to understanding a generation that is reshaping how we think, speak, and connect. In the pages that follow, we'll break down the slang you need to know, explain how and when to use it, and provide you with the tools to speak confidently, without feeling like an outsider. This guide will demystify Gen Z's language, teaching you not only the words but also the cultural context behind them. It's about more than just memorizing phrases—it's about understanding what they mean in the grander scheme of human connection.

Who is Gen Z?

If you don't know much about Gen Z, you're not alone. In many ways, they've slipped under the radar of mainstream conversation. And yet, they're the first generation to grow up entirely in the digital age. They've seen the world change rapidly, from the rise of social media to the explosion of streaming platforms.

Gen Z is tech-savvy, creative, and highly attuned to the world around them. They're often ahead of the curve when it comes to adopting new technologies and exploring new trends. They don't just consume culture—they shape it. From viral TikTok dances to meme-driven humor, their influence is all around us.

But it's not just their tech skills that set them apart. Gen Z has a unique worldview. They are more socially conscious than previous generations, prioritizing mental health, inclusivity, and sustainability. This generation is quick to spot trends, challenge the status quo, and create a language that reflects these values. For them, communication is a tool for self-expression, empowerment, and, most importantly, connection.

Why Slang? Why Does It Matter?

Here's the thing: slang isn't new. It's been around as long as humans have communicated. Every generation develops its own way of speaking, its own set of codes, that helps create group identity. But what makes Gen Z's slang so different is its speed, its pervasiveness, and its digital roots. Words and phrases can rise and fall in a matter of weeks, and with social media amplifying trends, what's cool today might be forgotten tomorrow. It's a fast-paced, fluid, and often unpredictable linguistic landscape.

And yet, this is exactly why slang matters.

Slang helps us communicate more efficiently, more emotionally, and more authentically. It's not just about shortening words or replacing formal terms; it's about capturing the mood, the energy, the feeling of the moment. When someone says, "That's lit," they're not just saying something is good—they're sharing excitement, joy, or enthusiasm in a way that feels more personal, more immediate.

But for those outside the loop, slang can feel like a wall, one that separates them from understanding what's really going on. This book is here to break down that wall.

In these pages, you will find a comprehensive guide to Gen Z's most commonly used slang, a key to unlocking the phrases that have become the language of today's youth. But we're not stopping there. We'll show you how to use them, when to use them, and—just as importantly—how to avoid using them in the wrong context. We'll also dive into the cultural significance behind each phrase, helping you understand why these words matter and how they reflect Gen Z's values.

By the end of this book, you'll no longer feel like you're on the outside looking in. You'll know how to speak Gen Z fluently—whether it's in the workplace, at a social gathering, or even in a family conversation. But more importantly, you'll understand how language shapes relationships and why it's essential to speak the language of the younger generation.

So, buckle up. The journey into the world of Gen Z slang starts here—and trust me, it's going to be a ride.

Chapter 1

The Rise of Gen Z Slang

Language is a living, breathing thing. It evolves with the times, shaped by the culture, the technology, and the collective spirit of each generation. In today's world, no generation has redefined language as boldly and as rapidly as Gen Z. This chapter explores how the slang that has emerged from this vibrant group is more than just a collection of quirky words—it's a reflection of their unique identity, their values, and their undeniable influence on the digital landscape. From TikTok challenges to meme culture, Gen Z's lexicon is quickly becoming a global force, and understanding it is key to bridging the gap between generations.

As we explore the roots of Gen Z slang, we'll uncover how it spread like wildfire, fueled by the power of social media, and how it reshapes our ideas about communication. What might seem like nonsense to some is, in fact, a coded language—one that speaks to the experiences, frustrations, and dreams of a generation growing up in the age of instant connectivity.

Historical Context

Language has always been a mirror of its time, evolving with the rhythms of society, culture, and technology. From the days when Baby Boomers coined their own expressions, like "groovy" or "far out," to the way Millennials popularized terms like "lit" or "on fleek," each generation's slang has been a reflection of their worldview, experiences, and the social forces shaping their lives.

However, nothing has accelerated the evolution of language quite like the internet. The digital age brought with it an explosion of communication methods—social media platforms, instant messaging, and texting—allowing language to spread faster than ever before. Where once it could take years for a new phrase to infiltrate popular culture, now it can take mere days, thanks to the viral nature of online platforms. This speed has created a language that is far more dynamic and ever-changing, with terms gaining traction, morphing, and sometimes fading away in the blink of an eye.

But it wasn't just the speed that changed things; it was the shift in how people communicate. The Baby Boomers grew up in an era where face-to-face interactions were the norm, and slang was passed along in person—through friends, family, or even television. In contrast, Gen Z has grown up in an interconnected world where communication is instant and constant. Social media platforms like Twitter, Instagram, and TikTok play a central role in their daily lives, and these platforms have become breeding grounds for new slang. The evolution of language is now dictated by algorithms and trending hashtags, where a phrase or a meme can explode into global usage overnight.

The advent of mobile texting further intensified these shifts, introducing shorthand abbreviations and acronyms—words like "lol," "brb," and "smh" became staples of digital dialogue. These weren't just time-savers; they were reinventions of how we express ourselves, driven by the need for brevity and speed in an increasingly fast-paced world.

With each new platform and technological development, language continued to adapt. Emojis, GIFs, and memes have become their own forms of communication, often more powerful than words themselves. What was once a simple letter or symbol now conveys an entire range of emotions, ideas, or humor in a way that words alone can't.

And now, in the era of Gen Z, the power of language is at its peak. With millions of young people using platforms like TikTok to not only communicate but also create trends, challenges, and movements, slang has become more than just a way to speak—it's a cultural currency.

It's how they define their identities, bond with each other, and set themselves apart from previous generations. The digital age has made slang more vital than ever, and understanding it is no longer optional. It's essential.

In the following sections, we will take a closer look at how Gen Z's language has evolved, how it connects them, and why understanding these terms has become crucial for anyone who wants to communicate effectively with this generation.

The Role of TikTok

In the world of social media, TikTok reigns supreme, particularly among Gen Z. With its fast-paced, video-centric platform, TikTok has become the epicenter of not just viral dances and challenges, but also of language innovation. For young people, TikTok isn't just a source of entertainment—it's a cultural force that shapes how they communicate, share ideas, and express themselves. Every day, millions of videos are posted, with new slang emerging almost overnight, often rising to global recognition with incredible speed.

TikTok's algorithm, which prioritizes trending content based on user interaction rather than traditional follower counts, has played a key role in this phenomenon. Unlike

Instagram or Twitter, where trends may take longer to catch on, TikTok thrives on virality. If a video uses a new term, phrase, or meme, it can be shared, remixed, and reinterpreted by millions within hours. Because of this, slang terms born on TikTok often travel from one corner of the globe to the other, crossing cultural, linguistic, and even national boundaries.

This viral ecosystem has made it easier than ever for new language to take hold. Take, for example, the phrase "no cap," which originated in hip-hop culture but gained massive popularity through TikTok. It now functions as an expression meaning "no lie" or "seriously." One catchy video using the phrase was all it took for it to become mainstream, adopted by millions of teens and young adults across the world. Such phrases gain traction not only because they are catchy or humorous, but because they're integrated into an ever-growing network of social media trends.

TikTok also fosters a sense of in-group identity. By adopting certain phrases or terms, users feel connected to others who share the same cultural references. Language becomes a marker of belonging, and the more niche or obscure the slang, the more coveted it becomes. It's not just about communication anymore—it's about identity and culture. If you understand the language of TikTok, you are in the know. If you don't, you risk being left behind.

Even more interesting is how TikTok has fueled the growth of global slang. Terms like "sus" (short for "suspicious") and "slaps" (meaning something is excellent, usually referring to music) have crossed from American English into other languages and dialects. TikTok's global reach has enabled slang to transcend borders in a way that was never possible before. In fact, slang terms from different countries and cultures are constantly finding their way into global conversations, blending in a unique way that reflects the cultural melting pot of social media.

It's not just about the videos themselves; it's the interaction with them that drives language evolution. TikTok users aren't just passive viewers—they engage with the content by commenting, remixing videos, and creating their own interpretations. This constant remixing allows slang to take on new meanings and nuances. A term might start as a joke in one video, but as users build on it, it evolves into a widely accepted part of everyday language. For instance, memes and catchphrases often start in niche subcultures on TikTok but gradually become part of the mainstream lexicon, thanks to this rapid interaction.

In short, TikTok isn't just a platform for sharing videos—it's a cultural incubator where new words, expressions, and ways of speaking are born and tested in real time. This has fundamentally altered how language spreads, making it more dynamic and ephemeral than ever before. For Gen Z, language on TikTok isn't just a means of communication—it's a part of their identity, a way to connect with others, and a tool for influencing culture. Understanding TikTok and its role in the evolution of slang is essential for anyone wanting to grasp the true essence of how Gen Z communicates today.

Key Influences on Gen Z Slang

The creation of Gen Z slang is deeply influenced by a complex mix of memes, internet culture, and youth subcultures, all of which play a critical role in shaping how language evolves. In this hyperconnected age, where cultural influences can spread like wildfire, Gen Z has embraced the power of the internet to craft a language uniquely their own. Memes, viral videos, gaming lexicon, and various subcultures all contribute to the slang that defines this generation's way of speaking.

Memes and Internet Culture

At the heart of Gen Z slang lies internet culture, which has become a breeding ground for the creation and spread of new terms and phrases. Memes, with their short, often humorous content, serve as both entertainment and a rapid-fire means of communication. What begins as an inside joke or a funny observation in a meme can quickly turn into a mainstream catchphrase that transcends its original context.

A prime example of this is the term "Yeet." What started as a meme—often accompanied by videos of people enthusiastically throwing something—became a catch-all word for expressing excitement, approval, or even just throwing something with force. Memes like these create a shared cultural language that unites users online, with certain phrases taking on a life of their own, morphing in meaning as they are passed around.

The Role of Subcultures

Subcultures, from skateboarding to gaming to K-pop fandoms, are also key influences in shaping Gen Z slang. Each of these subcultures has its own unique lexicon, but the beauty of Gen Z's use of slang lies in its ability to blend these diverse influences into a larger cultural conversation.

For instance, the gaming community has long had its own vocabulary, with terms like "GG" (Good Game), "AFK" (Away From Keyboard), or "Lag" crossing over into mainstream slang. Many of these gaming terms have become so ingrained in everyday speech that they no longer require knowledge of the gaming world to understand. They're simply part of Gen Z's broader communication toolkit.

The world of hip-hop and rap culture has similarly shaped much of Gen Z's language, contributing phrases like "no cap" (meaning "no lie" or "for real"), "slaps" (referring to music that is great), and "lit" (used to describe something exciting or impressive). These phrases, once popularized by artists and their fans, now flow seamlessly into casual conversations, transcending their original contexts.

Even fashion, particularly the rise of streetwear and sneaker culture, contributes to the evolution of language. Terms like "drip" (referring to stylish or fashionable clothing) and "flex" (to show off) have crossed over from these spaces, making their way into daily conversations and social media posts.

Global Influences and Linguistic Blending

One of the most fascinating aspects of Gen Z slang is the blending of linguistic influences from around the globe. With the rise of global platforms like TikTok, Instagram, and YouTube, Gen Z is exposed to a melting pot of languages, dialects, and cultural references. The borders of traditional language have blurred, creating a more inclusive and diverse vocabulary.

Words and phrases from different countries and cultures now seamlessly enter the lexicon, often without the original speakers realizing it. For example, "salty," meaning to be bitter or upset, was originally a term from African American Vernacular English (AAVE), but now it's widely used in both the U.S. and abroad. Similarly, expressions like "savage," once tied to specific cultural contexts, have become part of the global vernacular, used to describe something or someone who is bold, unbothered, or fierce.

The influence of non-English languages is also evident. In the U.S., terms like "churro" (borrowed from Spanish), "chill" (from both the American and Latin American slang) and "fam" (originally rooted in AAVE, now adopted by many different cultures) have made their way into daily conversations. Gen Z is not only influenced by the slang of their immediate peers but also by the language of the wider world, creating a hybridized, global dialect.

Blending Pop Culture

In addition to youth subcultures and internet memes, pop culture plays a huge role in shaping Gen Z slang. Movies, TV shows, music, and celebrity behavior provide endless inspiration for new words and phrases. For example, phrases like "Vibe check," which emerged from online meme culture and was popularized by influencers and TikTok stars, have quickly become a part of the everyday Gen Z lexicon. This blending of entertainment, media, and social influence has given Gen Z a truly dynamic and fast-evolving language.

The rapid pace at which new trends and slang emerge means that Gen Z has an incredibly fluid approach to language. What is "lit" today might be "mid" (mediocre) tomorrow, reflecting how quickly new words can spread across the digital landscape. It's a constant cycle of creation, adaptation, and reinvention, where language is both a reflection of and a driver for cultural change. This fluidity makes Gen Z's slang so unique and so tied to the ever-changing rhythms of digital culture.

Ultimately, the key influences on Gen Z slang create a tapestry of diverse linguistic elements, each shaping how they communicate with each other and with the world. Memes, internet culture, youth subcultures, global influences, and pop culture all combine to form a language that is as innovative as it is inclusive. For anyone looking to understand how Gen Z communicates, it's essential to grasp the many factors that influence their vocabulary—and to recognize that, just as they shape the language, they too are shaped by it.

The rise of Gen Z slang isn't just a passing trend; it's a cultural shift that's here to stay. What began as playful banter on social media has evolved into a way for Gen Z to express their individuality, assert their views, and create an online identity that resonates with others. Slang is more than just shorthand for the digital age; it's a tool for connection, a way for a generation to claim their space in a world that's increasingly driven by technology and rapid change. As we move through this book, we'll discover how to not only understand these terms but use them with confidence and authenticity, ensuring that communication—whether with Gen Z or across generations—remains rich, meaningful, and relevant.

Chapter 2

Breaking Down Common Gen Z Slang Terms

In the fast-paced world of Gen Z, slang terms come and go in the blink of an eye, with each new phrase reflecting the ever-changing trends, attitudes, and behaviors of this dynamic generation. Understanding these terms is more than just a linguistic exercise—it's a window into how Gen Z thinks, communicates, and connects with each other in an increasingly digital and interconnected world. In this chapter, we'll break down some of the most common Gen Z slang terms, exploring their meanings, origins, and how to use them correctly. Whether you're trying to decode the latest TikTok trend or simply connect with younger generations, this guide will help you navigate the rich, diverse world of Gen Z's language.

The Essential Vocabulary

Gen Z slang can feel like a secret code to those outside of the generation, but with a little context and understanding, it becomes a tool for deeper connection and communication. In this section, we'll break down some of the most popular and widely used Gen Z slang terms, providing clear definitions, examples of how to use them, and an exploration of how these terms vary by region or trend. Each entry will include a tier ranking to show how widely each term is used, helping you navigate the ever-evolving world of Gen Z slang.

1. Lit

- Definition: Something that's exciting, fun, or excellent.
- Context and Usage Examples:
    - "That party was so lit last night!"
    - "This new album is straight-up lit."
- Variations/Regional Differences: "Lit" is widely used across the U.S. and in other English-speaking countries but has gained more traction in urban and youth culture, especially in music and entertainment.
- Popularity Ranking: A-tier—A highly popular term, often used in mainstream media.

2. Stan

- Definition: To be a very passionate fan of someone or something. Derived from the Eminem song "Stan," which tells the story of an obsessed fan.
- Context and Usage Examples:

- - "I stan Billie Eilish—she's the best!"
  - "I can't stop watching this show; I stan it so hard."
- Variations/Regional Differences: While the term is primarily used in English-speaking countries, "stan" is universal in fan communities online, particularly in music and celebrity culture.
- Popularity Ranking: A-tier—A staple of fan culture, used widely on platforms like Twitter and Instagram.

3. Slay

- Definition: To do something exceptionally well, or to look stunning. Often used in reference to fashion or personal achievements.
- Context and Usage Examples:
  - "You're slaying that outfit today!"
  - "She totally slayed her performance at the concert."
- Variations/Regional Differences: Common in the LGBTQ+ community, but it has permeated mainstream use, particularly in fashion and beauty culture.
- Popularity Ranking: A-tier—Used regularly across social media platforms, especially Instagram and TikTok.

4. Bet

- Definition: A term used to express agreement or confirmation, similar to saying "okay" or "I got you." Can also be used to imply a challenge or a promise.
- Context and Usage Examples:
  - "You wanna go to the beach? Bet."
  - "You think you can beat me at that game? Bet."
- Variations/Regional Differences: While the term is used across the U.S., it is most prevalent in urban slang and hip-hop culture.
- Popularity Ranking: B-tier—Widely used but can be niche in certain contexts, especially within specific friend groups or communities.

5. Cap/No Cap

- Definition: "Cap" means to lie, and "no cap" means to tell the truth or to be serious.
- Context and Usage Examples:
  - "That's cap; didn't really meet Drake."
  - "I'm serious, no cap, I got straight A's this semester."
- Variations/Regional Differences: "Cap" and "no cap" are heavily used in urban communities and hip-hop culture, but their popularity has spread to the mainstream through memes and viral trends.
- Popularity Ranking: A-tier—A major part of modern internet slang, commonly used on platforms like TikTok and Twitter.

6. FOMO

- Definition: Fear of Missing Out—anxiety about missing an experience or event that others are enjoying.
- Context and Usage Examples:
    - "I couldn't make it to the party, and now I'm feeling major FOMO."
    - "I didn't go to the concert last night and I'm still dealing with the FOMO."
- Variations/Regional Differences: While "FOMO" originated in the U.S., it has become a global term, especially in the context of social media.
- Popularity Ranking: A-tier—Commonly used in both casual conversations and articles, especially related to social media and online culture.

7. Ghosting

- Definition: The act of suddenly cutting off all communication with someone without explanation, particularly in relationships or dating.
- Context and Usage Examples:
    - "We were texting for weeks, then he just ghosted me."
    - "Don't be that person who ghosts someone after a date."
- Variations/Regional Differences: Ghosting is largely a phenomenon that grew with online

dating and social media. It's widely used in English-speaking countries, though the act itself is global.

- Popularity Ranking: B-tier—Still widely used but often linked specifically to the world of online dating and friendships.

8. Yeet

- Definition: To throw something with force or enthusiasm. It can also express excitement or approval.
- Context and Usage Examples:
    - "I yeeted that bottle across the room.
    - "Yeet! This party is gonna be so much fun!"
- Variations/Regional Differences: While "yeet" originated as internet slang, it has made its way into everyday conversations, especially among younger people and in the context of playful actions.
- Popularity Ranking: C-tier—While once incredibly popular, the term is now a bit more niche and used for humor, especially in meme culture.

9. Vibe

- Definition: A term used to describe the overall feeling or atmosphere of a situation, person, or place. It can refer to a positive or negative energy.
- Context and Usage Examples:
    - "The vibe at this party is amazing!"

- ○ "She's giving off some bad vibes today."
- Variations/Regional Differences: "Vibe" has been adopted across many cultures, especially in music and social media spaces. While widely used, it can sometimes be more common in specific subcultures like music or spirituality.
- Popularity Ranking: A-tier—A versatile term used in many contexts, from casual conversations to deep discussions about emotions or environments.

10. Flex

- Definition: To show off, often in a boastful way, whether it's about wealth, accomplishments, or personal possessions.
- Context and Usage Examples:
    - ○ "He's always flexing his new car on Instagram."
    - ○ "I'm not here to flex, but I just got a promotion!"
- Variations/Regional Differences: "Flex" has been a popular term in hip-hop culture but has spread widely in social media circles. Its use is often tied to materialism or self-promotion, particularly in the context of influencers and celebrities.
- Popularity Ranking: B-tier—Still prevalent, but often seen as a bit of a stereotype or used humorously.

These are just a handful of the most popular terms currently used in Gen Z's vocabulary. As with any evolving language, new slang is born every day, and older terms may fade in favor of fresh phrases. However, these terms provide a glimpse into how Gen Z uses language not only to communicate but also to express identity, creativity, and belonging in an increasingly digital world. Understanding and adopting these terms will help bridge communication gaps and create stronger connections with younger generations.

Examples to Include

"Cap" / "No Cap"
- Definition: "Cap" refers to a lie or something that's untrue, while "No Cap" means you're being truthful or serious.

Example:
- "Bro, you're capping!"
- "No cap, I'm telling the truth."
- Context and Usage: The use of "cap" has exploded in recent years, particularly among Gen Z. It's often used to call out exaggeration or deception. On the flip side, "no cap" is used to emphasize honesty, making it the perfect way to assert credibility or truthfulness in a conversation.

- Popularity Ranking: A-tier. Widely used across various social media platforms, including TikTok and Twitter.

"Bet"

- Definition: A term used to express agreement or affirmation, similar to saying "OK" or "I'm in." It can also be used to accept a challenge or to confirm plans.

Example:

- "Wanna go to the mall?"

"Bet."

- Context and Usage: "Bet" is casual and direct, often used in friendly or informal settings. It can be used when making plans, accepting an invitation, or even making lighthearted bets or challenges. It's an expression of readiness and enthusiasm.
- Popularity Ranking: B-tier. Popular in urban and youth cultures, particularly within tight-knit groups of friends.

"Slay"

- Definition: To do something exceptionally well or to look stunning, often used in reference to fashion, performance, or success.

Example:

- "You slayed that performance!"
- "She's slaying in that dress."

- Context and Usage: "Slay" has evolved from its roots in drag culture to become a mainstream term used to compliment someone's abilities or appearance. It conveys admiration for someone who's performing or presenting themselves exceptionally well, whether it's in terms of fashion, attitude, or achievement.
- Popularity Ranking: A-tier. Commonly used in pop culture, especially on Instagram and other platforms focused on fashion and self-expression.

"Lit"

- Definition: Describes something that is exciting, fun, or excellent. Often used in reference to parties, events, or experiences that are particularly enjoyable or memorable.

Example:

- "That party was lit!"
- "The concert was lit, we had such a great time!"
- Context and Usage: "Lit" has been a staple in Gen Z's vocabulary for years, often used to describe high-energy events, fun gatherings, or anything that's considered "cool" or exciting. Its usage has been carried forward from the previous generation, but it continues to evolve and remain relevant in modern youth culture.
- Popularity Ranking: A-tier. Still widely used across social media platforms and in casual conversation.

"Bet" vs. "Bop"

- Definition: Both terms can describe something positive, but their usage and meaning differ in subtle ways. "Bet" is an expression of agreement or confirmation, whereas "bop" refers to a catchy song or something that is fun and upbeat.

Example for *"Bet"*:

- "You want to hit the movies?"

"Bet."

Example for "Bop":

- "This song is a straight-up bop!"
- "That new album is full of bops."
- Context and Usage: "Bet" is often used in casual agreements or affirmations, while "bop" is usually reserved for music or anything with a good rhythm or vibe. Though both terms convey positive energy, "bet" is more about mutual agreement, whereas "bop" expresses enjoyment or admiration for a musical piece or a situation that gives off positive energy.
- Popularity Ranking:

"Bet": B-tier

- "Bop": B-tier—Both are popular, but "bop" is more confined to music and specific contexts, whereas "bet" is used in a broader variety of situations.

"Vibe" and "Vibing"

- Definition: "Vibe" refers to the general feeling, atmosphere, or energy of a situation, event, or person. "Vibing" is the act of experiencing or being in tune with that vibe, often in a relaxed or enjoyable way.

Example:

- "I'm just vibing right now."
- "This café has a great vibe."
- Context and Usage: "Vibe" has become one of the most versatile and frequently used Gen Z terms. It can describe anything from the mood of a party to the ambiance of a place or even a person's personality. "Vibing" is often used to indicate that someone is going with the flow, enjoying the moment, or feeling the energy of their surroundings.
- Popularity Ranking: A-tier. Ubiquitous across various platforms and social settings, particularly on Instagram and TikTok where people share moments that evoke strong emotions or feelings.

These terms represent just a snapshot of the vibrant and dynamic vocabulary that Gen Z has developed. As language continues to evolve, these words not only serve as a means of communication but also as tools for expressing individuality, humor, and belonging. By understanding and using this slang, individuals of all generations can better connect with younger audiences, offering a bridge between cultures and fostering deeper connections.

As we've seen, the language of Gen Z is an ever-evolving mix of creativity, humor, and social awareness. Each slang term carries with it not just a definition, but a reflection of the culture, values, and experiences that shape this generation. By understanding the meanings behind these terms and how they fit into the larger cultural conversation, you'll be better equipped to communicate effectively and authentically with Gen Z. In the next chapter, we'll explore how to incorporate these terms into your own vocabulary, making them feel natural and meaningful in everyday conversations.

Chapter 3

How to Use Gen Z Slang Effectively

Gen Z slang isn't just a passing trend—it's a language that reflects a unique way of thinking, interacting, and expressing identity. But knowing the slang is only part of the equation; using it effectively is what really connects you with this generation. This chapter will explore the dos and don'ts of integrating Gen Z slang into your everyday conversations, ensuring you're not just using the words, but using them the right way. By the end, you'll understand how to incorporate these terms with authenticity, respect, and confidence—helping you build stronger connections with the younger generation and communicate with the fluidity they expect.

Using Slang in Conversation

Integrating Gen Z slang into your everyday conversations requires more than just knowing the words—it's about understanding when and how to use them naturally. Using slang authentically is key to connecting with younger generations, but it's also important to avoid sounding like you're trying too hard. The goal is to make the language feel like an extension of your regular speech, not a forced addition.

To help you navigate this, let's break down how to use Gen Z slang in a way that feels both effortless and organic.

1. Know the Right Context

Using slang correctly begins with understanding its context. Gen Z slang isn't just a list of words—it's a reflection of the culture and energy behind them. When you use slang, ask yourself: Does this fit the situation? Does it reflect the mood or energy of the conversation? If you're talking about something exciting or fun, using terms like "lit" or "vibe" can elevate the energy. On the other hand, using "bet" to confirm plans or "cap" to call out lies feels much more natural in a casual conversation.

2. Avoid Overuse

One of the most important things to remember when using Gen Z slang is to avoid overloading your speech with too many terms. Just like any language, slang can lose its effect if used too frequently or inappropriately. Imagine trying to use "slay" in every sentence—it would quickly feel forced and out of place. A good rule of thumb is to use slang sparingly to keep it fresh and impactful. Pick your moments, and use the terms when they make sense.

Examples of Good vs. Bad Usage

Let's look at two contrasting examples to see how Gen Z slang can be used effectively versus awkwardly.

Good Usage Example:

You're hanging out with a friend who's just completed a difficult project, and you're impressed by their work.

You: "Yo, that presentation was fire! You really slayed it. Honestly, I don't think anyone could have done it better."
Friend: "Thanks! I was nervous, but I'm glad it came out good."
You: "No cap, it was awesome. You really put in the work, and it shows."

Here, the use of fire, slayed, and no cap fits the energy of the conversation. You're acknowledging your friend's accomplishment, and these terms feel natural because they reflect your genuine enthusiasm and admiration. The slang flows smoothly with the tone and context of the conversation.

Bad Usage Example:

Imagine you're at a formal work meeting, discussing the quarterly reports with your boss.

You: "Yo, these numbers are lit—like, straight up, vibing at a whole new level. No cap, this quarter's performance is fire!"
Boss: "I see. But I would appreciate it if we could focus on the details of the report."
You: "Bet, bet—I'll just say, the report's slaying it, you know?"

In this scenario, the use of slang like lit, vibing, and fire is out of place. The casual tone doesn't match the formal context of a work meeting. Using slang here would not only sound forced but could undermine your professionalism. In this setting, it's better to keep your language clear and concise, without relying on slang to communicate your point.

3. Gauge Your Audience

It's also essential to gauge your audience before using Gen Z slang. What works with friends or peers may not fly with family members or in more professional settings. Take time to understand the cultural background and comfort level of your listeners. Some slang may be widely understood, while others may be niche, and it's important to use terms that your audience will recognize and appreciate.

For example, using "bet" or "cap" may resonate well with a group of younger individuals who are active on social media platforms, but older generations or those not in tune with TikTok trends may not understand the terms as easily. In these cases, it's a good idea to either introduce the terms gently or avoid them entirely.

4. Authenticity Over Mimicry

Perhaps the most important aspect of using Gen Z slang is authenticity. If the slang doesn't feel natural to you, don't force it. Forcing yourself to use terms you don't feel comfortable with will likely come across as inauthentic. Instead, pick a few terms that resonate with your personality and style of communication and integrate them gradually. Slang should feel like an addition to your vocabulary, not an imitation of another group's speech patterns.

Final Tip: Keep it cool, keep it casual. Gen Z's slang thrives in relaxed, informal settings where the goal is to communicate and connect. If you're unsure about a term, test it out with a friend or group who understands it, and see how it feels. The more you engage with the language, the more naturally it will integrate into your conversations.

In sum, using Gen Z slang effectively isn't about memorizing a list of words; it's about knowing when, where, and how to use them so that they come across naturally. With the right balance, these terms can enhance your conversations and allow you to communicate with the younger generation in an authentic, relatable way. Whether you're keeping up with trends or simply trying to connect with a younger friend or colleague, understanding how to use slang properly is a valuable skill in today's evolving linguistic landscape.

Slang in Professional Settings

As language continues to evolve, many people wonder if it's okay to use slang in professional environments—particularly Gen Z slang. The answer isn't always straightforward, and knowing when and how to use slang at work can make a significant difference in how you're perceived by colleagues and clients, especially those from different age groups. Gen Z slang has become an integral part of the modern lexicon, but integrating it into professional settings requires a nuanced approach. Here's how to navigate it.

When It's Okay to Use Slang

In some professional settings, using Gen Z slang can actually help build stronger connections. Younger generations, particularly Gen Z, often prefer a more casual, relaxed communication style, especially in workplaces with a younger, tech-savvy demographic. Here are the instances where using slang can work in your favor:

- Building Rapport with Younger Colleagues or Clients: If you're working in a creative industry, tech startup, or any environment that's culturally tuned into current trends, using Gen Z slang can show that you're relatable and in sync with the current cultural climate. It can help build a sense of camaraderie and break down barriers, particularly with younger colleagues or clients who appreciate when others speak their "language."

- Example: If you're leading a meeting with a Gen Z colleague who just completed a challenging project, saying "You really slayed that presentation!" can acknowledge their success while reinforcing your connection through shared language.

- Casual and Collaborative Environments: If the work environment is relaxed and everyone tends to have a more informal style of communication (for example, in tech or marketing), using slang can add to the overall culture of the workplace. This can create a feeling of inclusivity, where everyone feels like they're part of the same team, especially when you're working together on projects that involve creativity or innovation.

- In Creative Presentations or Team Brainstorms: In brainstorming sessions or more informal work settings, using slang to express excitement or enthusiasm can help energize a team. Words like "lit," "fire," and "vibe" can capture the energy and emotion behind creative ideas, making the discussion feel more dynamic.

Example: "This idea is fire! I'm really vibing with it." This shows passion for the project and engages your team in a more expressive way.

When It's Not Okay to Use Slang

While slang can be powerful in some professional contexts, there are also clear boundaries when it comes to its use in formal settings or situations where clarity, professionalism, and respect are paramount. Here are some instances where you should avoid using Gen Z slang:

- Formal Communications: In emails, presentations, or formal reports, using slang can come across as unprofessional and reduce your credibility. Slang can undermine the seriousness of the communication, making you seem less authoritative or even juvenile.

Example: Using terms like "Bet" or "Cap" in a client proposal or during a formal presentation could confuse your audience or distract from the point you're trying to make.

- Leadership Roles: If you're in a leadership or managerial position, it's important to set a tone of respect and authority. While casual interactions are fine, overusing slang could undermine your role as a leader. For example, addressing a senior executive with, "Yo, no cap, this report is fire," might not convey the level of professionalism expected in the situation.

- Cross-Generational Communication: In situations where you're communicating with older generations (e.g., Baby Boomers or Gen X) who may not be familiar with Gen Z slang, it's better to stick to clear and formal language. Using slang in these instances may confuse your audience and alienate them from the conversation. If you want to connect with someone from a different generation, it's essential to gauge their comfort level with informal language and adjust your communication style accordingly.

How Gen Z Slang Can Help Build Rapport

When used correctly, slang can be a powerful tool to foster connections and strengthen relationships. If you're working with younger colleagues or clients, incorporating slang can make you seem more approachable, down-to-earth, and understanding of their cultural references. It helps bridge the generational divide by showing that you're in tune with their world.

For example, saying "That's lit" when reacting to a new idea or showing genuine interest in a conversation can signal that you're open, enthusiastic, and ready to engage. It makes interactions feel less stiff and more conversational. However, this doesn't mean overusing slang or relying on it entirely to communicate—its effectiveness lies in its subtlety and timeliness.

The Risks of Overusing Slang in Professional Communication

While a little slang can go a long way, overusing it in professional settings can have serious consequences. Here are some of the risks associated with using too much slang in your work life:

- Undermining Your Professionalism: Excessive use of slang, particularly in formal or serious discussions, can make you seem immature or unprofessional. Clients, bosses, or colleagues who aren't familiar with the slang may not take you seriously or may even question your competence. Professionalism in communication signals competence, maturity, and respect for the work and your audience.

- Misunderstanding and Confusion: Not everyone understands Gen Z slang, especially if they're not active on social media or digital platforms. Overusing slang can create confusion, causing colleagues or clients to misunderstand your message or miss key points. This can lead to mistakes, delays, or miscommunication, particularly in high-stakes situations.

Example: If you're presenting a marketing strategy to a client and you say, "We need to make sure this campaign is vibing with the audience," the client might not understand what you mean, even though it's clear to your peers.

- Alienation: Overuse of slang can also alienate certain groups within your workplace. It may create a sense of exclusion, particularly for older or less familiar colleagues, who might feel left out of the conversation. This can diminish the inclusivity of a team or make someone feel like they're out of touch. It's essential to balance informal language with respect for the diversity of language preferences within a team.

Using Gen Z slang in professional settings can be a valuable tool for building rapport and fostering a sense of connection with younger colleagues or clients. However, it's essential to be mindful of the context and to know when and where it's appropriate. The key is to strike a balance between professionalism and relatability—using slang to enhance communication without letting it detract from the message you're trying to convey. By learning to navigate these nuances, you can communicate effectively across generations and ensure that you're always using language in a way that aligns with your professional environment.

Overcoming the Fear of Sounding "Old"

One of the most common concerns for individuals from older generations when it comes to using Gen Z slang is the fear of sounding "out of touch" or "old." The rapid evolution of language, especially in the digital age, can make it challenging to stay current, and the fear of misusing slang can make people hesitant to try it at all. However, embracing new language and communication styles doesn't have to be daunting. In fact, with the right mindset and approach, anyone can confidently incorporate slang into their vocabulary—without overthinking or worrying about looking out of place.

Here's how to overcome the fear of using slang and feel more confident in your language skills:

1. Start Slow and Observe

The first step is to start small. You don't need to dive headfirst into every new slang term you hear. Instead, take time to observe how younger people around you use slang—whether it's through social media, movies, or conversations. You can learn a lot just by listening to how the slang is naturally integrated into dialogue.

For example, watching TikToks or following influencers who use Gen Z slang in a natural, casual way can help you understand not only the meaning of the terms but also the tone and context in which they're used. By gradually incorporating a few terms you feel comfortable with, you'll avoid feeling overwhelmed by the sheer number of slang words out there.

2. Don't Try to Force It

When learning any new language or dialect, it's important to avoid forcing terms into your vocabulary just for the sake of it. Slang should feel organic and natural, not like an attempt to "fit in." Forcing slang into conversations, especially when it doesn't quite make sense, can come off as inauthentic or even awkward.

Rather than trying to use every term you learn, focus on incorporating a few expressions that genuinely resonate with you. If you're unsure, it's better to stick with words you've heard regularly and feel confident about using in the right context. If "slay" feels comfortable for you but "cap" doesn't quite land, that's perfectly fine.

3. Embrace Mistakes as Part of the Process

Fear of using a term incorrectly is one of the biggest barriers to adopting slang, but here's the truth: everyone makes mistakes. Even native speakers of slang might use a term wrong occasionally—especially with how quickly language shifts. If you accidentally use a term incorrectly, the key is to acknowledge the mistake in a way that feels natural.

For instance, if you say, "This party is lit!" and a younger colleague gently corrects you by saying, "Actually, it's more of a 'vibe,' not 'lit,'" embrace the moment with humor and openness. Something as simple as laughing it off and saying, "Ah, noted! I'm learning," can defuse the situation and show your willingness to connect rather than trying to sound "cool."

Remember, no one expects perfection when you're learning a new way of speaking. The fact that you're making the effort already sets you apart in a positive way.

4. Use Slang to Connect, Not Impress

One of the most important things to remember is that slang isn't about impressing others—it's about building connection. Whether you're talking to a colleague, a friend, or a client, using Gen Z slang can be a tool to relate to others, not just to "sound younger." People appreciate when someone makes an effort to engage in their language, especially when it's done in an authentic and relatable way.

Instead of worrying about whether you're using the slang correctly, focus on the connection you're creating by showing interest in how younger people express themselves. When you ask questions like "What does 'sus' mean again?" or "How do you use 'no cap' in a sentence?", you show curiosity and openness—qualities that are far more important than getting the slang exactly right.

5. Keep It Light and Fun

Finally, don't take it too seriously. Language, especially slang, is meant to be fun and playful. If you approach slang with a sense of humor and curiosity, it takes the pressure off. Laugh at your mistakes, ask questions when you're unsure, and enjoy the process of learning. The more relaxed you are, the more naturally you'll be able to use slang without overthinking it.

And even if you never fully master every new term, your willingness to embrace slang can still be a conversation starter. It shows that you're in touch with evolving trends and that you're not afraid to step outside your comfort zone. In turn, it can lead to richer, more engaging conversations with people from all walks of life.

The fear of sounding "old" is natural, but it shouldn't stop you from embracing new forms of expression. Language is a tool for connection, and Gen Z slang is simply another way to engage with the world around us. The key is to approach it with confidence, authenticity, and a willingness to learn. By observing, listening, and embracing the fun side of slang, you'll be able to incorporate it naturally into your conversations, build stronger connections across generations, and maybe even have a little fun along the way.

Mastering Gen Z slang isn't about mimicking their language—it's about embracing their culture and finding common ground. By following the guidelines in this chapter, you'll be able to speak their language without sounding forced or out of touch. Language is powerful, and when used correctly, Gen Z slang can be a bridge to understanding and connecting with this dynamic generation. Whether it's for personal relationships, professional settings, or just staying in the know, knowing how to use these words effectively will keep you relevant and in tune with the evolving world of communication.

Chapter 4

Slang to Avoid or Use Sparingly

While Gen Z slang can be a powerful tool for connecting with younger generations, not every term is universally embraced, and some slang words can quickly fall out of favor or be seen as inappropriate in certain settings. The popularity of slang tends to be fleeting, and what's cool today might not carry the same weight tomorrow. This chapter explores the types of slang to be cautious about using, offering insight into which terms might be better left out of your vocabulary—or used sparingly. Understanding the nuances of language is crucial to making sure you stay relevant without crossing into territory that could alienate or confuse your audience.

Slang That's Gone Too Far

Gen Z slang has rapidly evolved, with certain words becoming viral sensations, only to eventually fall victim to overuse or misuse. In some cases, what started as an edgy or humorous expression can quickly turn cringe-worthy or even inappropriate when used too often or in the wrong context. As with all trends, slang can burn bright but fade quickly, leaving some terms in the dust. Here, we explore a few of the most prominent examples of slang that has overstayed its welcome, providing insight into why they've gone too far and offering guidance on when, or if, they should be used.

"Mommy"

The term "mommy" has experienced a major transformation, particularly on platforms like TikTok. Originally a cute, endearing word used to describe one's mother, the term has been repurposed into a somewhat controversial slang term that carries a mix of playful flirtation and awkwardness. In the TikTok space, "mommy" has taken on a hypersexualized or fetishized connotation, often tied to "mommy kink" subcultures or used in an ironic, tongue-in-cheek way by younger users. While some Gen Zers may still use the term humorously or innocently, the term has become a polarizing one. For many, "mommy" no longer carries the warmth or affection it once did and has instead become a source of discomfort when used outside its traditional meaning.

Example:

- "Who's your mommy?" – In TikTok trends, this phrase has become more suggestive, losing its wholesome roots.

"Blood"

In the world of Gen Z slang, "blood" is a term that originally had ties to family, as in "my blood" or "blood brother." However, the term has grown in popularity in online spaces, especially in urban and rap culture, to refer to close friends or even to convey a sense of kinship in online groups. But here's where it gets tricky: as the term caught on, it began to be overused, especially in meme-based content and among influencers. As a result, "blood" has lost some of its original edge and, in some circles, can now come across as a forced attempt at fitting in. It's important to note that while "blood" is still a valid term in some contexts, it's best used sparingly to avoid sounding disingenuous or out of touch.

Example:
- "Yo, what's up blood?" – It can sound forced and inauthentic when used excessively or by people outside certain cultural circles.

"Ohio"

"Ohio" is a term that emerged as part of a meme-based trend, often referencing the state of Ohio in a bizarre or exaggerated context, and typically used to describe chaotic or surreal scenarios. The meme gained traction due to its absurdity, with videos and posts featuring Ohio being used as a shorthand for something that's "wild" or "strange." While this started as a quirky, humorous meme, the term has quickly become repetitive and, for many, tiresome. What was once an amusing exaggeration has now grown to the point of being overused and even irritating. In some instances, "Ohio" has been co-opted to mean any place or situation that's perceived as "weird," but as with many memes, its novelty has worn thin.

Example:
- "That party was like Ohio." – This comparison, once funny, is now so overused it has lost its original impact and charm.

Why These Terms Should Be Used Sparingly

While these terms may have once held a certain charm or humor, their overuse has led to a saturation point where they are no longer effective in conveying the intended tone or message. The rapid spread of slang via TikTok and other social platforms means that trends can go viral almost overnight, but they can also flame out just as quickly. When words like "mommy," "blood," and "Ohio" are overused, they risk alienating the very people they were meant to connect with. Using them excessively can make communication feel stale or disingenuous, especially when the terms have shifted away from their original meanings.

Understanding when a slang term has run its course is key to staying relevant in Gen Z communication. The ability to adapt and move away from outdated slang not only shows that you're in touch with evolving language trends, but it also demonstrates that you respect the fluid nature of culture. So, while it may be tempting to pepper your speech with terms that once got big laughs, it's often wiser to allow these terms to fade into the background and let new slang take their place.

Slang, by nature, is fluid and ever-changing. Terms like "mommy," "blood," and "Ohio" have crossed the line from fresh and edgy to overused and, in some cases, cringeworthy. By being mindful of how often these words are used and in what context, you can avoid sounding out of touch. When in doubt, it's often best to let certain terms rest and only bring them out when they truly feel authentic. As with all things linguistic, balance is key to ensuring your communication stays relevant and engaging.

When to Let Slang Die

Slang, by nature, is a reflection of the culture, energy, and mindset of a particular time. It evolves rapidly, shaping itself around trends, societal shifts, and technological advances. However, as quickly as slang can rise to prominence, it can also fall into obscurity. The lifespan of a slang term is often short-lived, and once it becomes overused, outdated, or too mainstream, it risks losing its original impact, leaving users sounding out of touch. Recognizing when to let slang die, or at least when to let it rest, is essential for staying relevant in modern communication.

The Natural Life Cycle of Slang

Every slang term has its own arc: it starts as a small, subcultural expression, gaining popularity as it's adopted by larger groups. Eventually, it can be overused, co-opted by mainstream media, or misused to the point that it loses its original meaning. At this point, it begins to fade into the background, replaced by new expressions that better capture the spirit of the times. This cycle is nothing new. From the "groovy" days of the 1960s to the "rad" and "awesome" era of the 1980s, slang terms rise and fall as quickly as the trends they represent.

In the digital age, this cycle happens even faster. With platforms like TikTok, Twitter, and Instagram, words can spread like wildfire and, just as quickly, lose their relevance. A term that once felt fresh can suddenly feel like a relic from the past when overused. Slang can age quickly, and its longevity is often tied to how authentically it reflects the culture it emerged from.

Why Some Slang Fades

Certain slang terms fade out over time for a few key reasons:

1. Overuse and Saturation: As a term becomes more popular, it can lose its punch. What once felt edgy and fun can become tired and cliché. Think of how "lit" once felt like the perfect descriptor for something exciting, only for it to become so ubiquitous that it eventually felt hollow and insincere.

2. Mainstream Adoption: When slang enters the mainstream, especially through commercial advertisements, influencers, or celebrities, it loses its edge. Terms that once belonged to specific subcultures or groups become overexposed and lose their authenticity. When everyone starts using a term, it's no longer the cool, underground expression it once was.

3. Misuse or Misinterpretation: Sometimes, a slang term falls out of favor because it's misused or misunderstood. This can happen when people outside the group that originally coined the term use it incorrectly, stripping it of its original meaning. For instance, when a term like "no cap" becomes ubiquitous, it risks losing its nuance and just sounds like filler in casual conversations.

4. Cultural Shifts: Slang often reflects the values and concerns of the time in which it's used. As cultural values shift, some terms may no longer fit. Words or phrases that were once empowering or playful can take on negative connotations, especially if they become associated with problematic trends or are used inappropriately.

The Impact of Using Outdated Slang

Using outdated or expired slang can have several negative effects, especially in communication.

1. Sounding Out of Touch: The most immediate consequence of using old slang is that you risk sounding out of touch. If you're still using terms from five years ago, it might give the impression that you're not in tune with the evolving cultural landscape, which could create a disconnect with your audience. The younger generation, particularly Gen Z, will likely notice when someone uses outdated slang, and it may impact your credibility.

2. Creating a Generational Divide: While some people may appreciate a nostalgic throwback to older slang, others will see it as a sign of not understanding the current lexicon. Older generations may feel more comfortable using slang they know, but it can come off as

trying too hard to fit in, potentially alienating younger audiences.

3. Decreasing Effectiveness: Slang loses its ability to convey the intended meaning or emotion when it becomes overused. It can lose its punch and, instead of adding flair or emphasis to a sentence, it may just sound forced. Communication becomes less effective when the terms you're using no longer resonate or add any value to the conversation.

4. Cultural Missteps: Using outdated slang can also lead to cultural missteps if the term has evolved in a way that no longer aligns with its original meaning or has become associated with something negative. In some cases, using a term that's been "canceled" or become problematic can make you appear insensitive or unaware of the evolving nature of language and culture.

When to Move On from Slang

Knowing when to move on from a slang term is an essential skill in maintaining effective communication. The key is to recognize when a word has overstayed its welcome and embrace the new lexicon as it develops. Here are a few indicators that it might be time to let a slang term die:

1. It's Everywhere: If the term has been widely adopted and is being used by a variety of people—especially those outside the cultural group that originated it—it's likely reached the point of saturation. When a term becomes commonplace, it often loses the originality and freshness that made it appealing in the first place.

2. It Feels Forced: If you're using a term because you feel like you "have to" or because everyone else is, rather than because it naturally fits into your vocabulary, it might be time to retire it. Authenticity is key in language, and using a term that doesn't feel organic will only make your communication sound contrived.

3. It No Longer Has the Same Impact: If the term is no longer delivering the same emotional punch or fun factor, it's a clear sign it might be time for it to fade. Slang only works when it's still fresh and has the ability to add something unique to the conversation. Once it's been overused, its power is diminished.

4. Cultural Sensitivity: If the term has become problematic or associated with something offensive, it's time to retire it from your vocabulary. Language evolves, and part of that evolution involves being aware of the cultural shifts that can affect how certain terms are perceived. It's important to stay aware of these changes and adjust accordingly.

Once it's clear that a particular slang term has run its course, the next step is to embrace new terms. This doesn't mean constantly chasing the latest trends, but rather staying open to how language evolves and being adaptable in your communication style. Engaging with Gen Z slang can be a fun and effective way to stay relevant and connect with younger generations, but it's important to be mindful of when certain terms need to be left behind.

Slang, much like fashion or music, is cyclical. What's in today might be out tomorrow, but that doesn't mean you can't continue to connect with others through fresh and exciting expressions. By letting go of outdated terms and embracing new ones, you stay current, relatable, and genuine in your communication. Language will continue to evolve, and so should the way we use it. The key is to balance being trendy with being authentic, so that you're always speaking the language of now—without sounding like you're trying too hard.

Using slang can enrich communication, but it requires awareness of context, timing, and the changing landscape of language. By being mindful of the slang that may have negative connotations or is simply out of touch, you can continue to engage in a way that feels both fresh and respectful. Knowing when to hold back from using certain terms or adjusting to evolving trends will ensure that your communication remains authentic, effective, and in tune with the times. Whether it's avoiding outdated slang or recognizing when to tone it down, navigating this aspect of language is key to fostering meaningful connections across generations.

Chapter 5

The Future of Gen Z Slang

As we stand on the brink of a new era in digital communication, the future of Gen Z slang seems both exciting and unpredictable. Language, after all, is never static; it constantly evolves, influenced by shifting cultural norms, technological advancements, and the ever-changing ways we connect with one another. While Gen Z's influence on modern slang has already made its mark, what lies ahead? How will the slang of today shape the conversations of tomorrow? In this chapter, we will explore the trajectory of Gen Z slang, how it may continue to evolve, and what future generations might inherit or redefine.

The Evolution of Slang

Slang is like a living organism—constantly evolving, adapting, and morphing to fit the times. Just as the culture and technology around us change, so too does the way we communicate. What's considered "cool" today might be outdated and cringeworthy tomorrow. In many ways, slang follows a predictable cycle: it emerges, gains popularity, and then fades into obscurity. However, some terms defy the typical path, sticking around longer than expected or even making a comeback after years of dormancy.

The process of slang evolution begins with a need for distinction—whether it's a way for youth to differentiate themselves from older generations, or an attempt to make a cultural statement. Slang is born in informal settings, typically among groups who are looking for new ways to express ideas, emotions, and experiences. These groups could be anything from subcultures and communities to global digital networks like TikTok. As new words or phrases catch on, they spread rapidly, amplified by the reach of social media and viral trends.

Once a term gains momentum, it enters its "peak" phase. During this time, it's used widely across various social groups and media platforms, becoming a core part of communication for the generation that popularized it. But the cycle doesn't stop there. Eventually, overuse and saturation lead to a decline in its novelty, and slang fades into the background. This phase is inevitable—once a term is widely adopted, it can lose its edge and may start to sound dated or forced.

However, not all slang follows this predictable trajectory. Some terms may resurface in different contexts or reemerge with a new twist, depending on the cultural climate. Others might evolve, merging with other phrases or adapting to new technologies and platforms. Even the terms that fade away may leave lasting impacts on language, influencing the creation of future slang.

Understanding the evolution of slang is crucial for anyone navigating today's linguistic landscape. The words and phrases that define one generation may become meaningless to the next, but they're all part of the same cycle of cultural expression. To stay relevant, it's important to recognize when slang is on the rise, how to incorporate it effectively, and when it's time to let go of terms that have passed their peak.

What's Next?

As we look ahead, the future of Gen Z slang remains both fascinating and unpredictable. The language of today's youth has already made an indelible mark on how we communicate, but what's next? What will the slang of tomorrow sound like, and how will it continue to evolve in the digital age?

One thing is certain: Gen Z's language is likely to remain deeply tied to technology, especially with the rapid growth of new platforms and the increasing impact of artificial intelligence, virtual reality, and other emerging tech. Just as TikTok played a central role in shaping the slang of today, it's easy to imagine that the next wave of slang will be influenced by newer social media trends, apps, and even new forms of virtual communication. The lines between the digital and physical world continue to blur, and this will undoubtedly shape how we express ourselves. Platforms like Discord, Clubhouse, and even newer forms of AI-powered interactions could contribute to the birth of even more niche or context-specific slang.

Additionally, the blending of different cultures—especially with global connectivity—will likely keep playing a key role in shaping language. Gen Z is increasingly multilingual and multicultural, pulling in influences from a wide array of global dialects, slang, and cultural movements. We can expect this fluidity to continue as borders become more irrelevant in the digital landscape. Slang may become even more inclusive and fluid, with terms and phrases crossing boundaries faster than ever before. This could lead to the creation of entirely new linguistic hybrids that draw on multiple languages or cultural references.

We might also see the further evolution of slang being more influenced by visuals than ever before. Emojis, GIFs, and memes are already a huge part of how Gen Z communicates, and in the future, slang might not even need to rely on words at all. Rather, these visual elements, which are already part of the everyday lexicon, could become more prominent. What starts as a visual trend—an emoji or a specific meme format—could evolve into an entire language shift. In this way, the future of slang may not only be spoken or written, but also visual, emotive, and multimodal, making communication even more immediate and expressive.

As for the trends we're seeing right now, some key areas may point the way toward the next wave of slang. One notable direction is the rise of AI and machine learning tools. With the development of tools that allow for conversational AI and virtual avatars, we could see an even greater integration of technology into the way slang is formed. As digital assistants, avatars, and bots become more mainstream, they might create entirely new linguistic needs and terms. Similarly, as the "metaverse" becomes more integrated into daily life, new digital spaces may bring about fresh terms that capture the nuances of virtual existence.

Another trend to keep an eye on is the increasing importance of environmental and social justice. As Gen Z continues to advocate for important causes—climate change, mental health awareness, and equity—we may see a new wave of slang that reflects these movements. Phrases that evoke activism or new ways of addressing societal issues could become mainstream, just as previous generations saw terms like "woke" and "cancel culture" gain traction.

The bottom line is that language, particularly slang, is always adapting to cultural, technological, and societal shifts. Just as Gen Z has shaped today's lexicon, they will continue to influence how we speak, write, and communicate in the future. Whether driven by viral trends, global influence, or new digital frontiers, the language of tomorrow is already taking shape—and Gen Z will undoubtedly be at the forefront, driving the next evolution in communication.

So, as we prepare to embrace what's next, one thing is clear: the journey of slang is far from over. If anything, it's just getting started.

The Role of Technology

As we look ahead, it's impossible to ignore the profound role that technology will play in shaping the future of language, particularly slang. Just as Gen Z's language has been heavily influenced by the rise of social media, smartphones, and platforms like TikTok, the next evolution of slang will likely be shaped by emerging technologies—particularly artificial intelligence (AI) and virtual reality (VR). These innovations could change not only how we communicate but also the very language we use.

AI and Language

Artificial intelligence is already revolutionizing many industries, and its influence on language is no exception. As AI becomes more advanced, its ability to understand, interpret, and even generate language is evolving at an exponential rate. This could lead to new forms of slang that are not only generated by humans but also by AI systems themselves.

One possibility is the development of "AI slang," which could emerge as virtual assistants, chatbots, and AI-driven social media platforms become more integrated into daily life. Imagine a world where we not only talk to each other using language but also communicate with AI in a way that introduces a new, hybrid form of slang. For example, AI might begin to incorporate phrases or idioms that sound odd or unique to human ears but are deeply ingrained in the AI's own programming logic. These terms could then enter the human lexicon, merging the digital and physical worlds in a completely new way.

Additionally, AI's role in automating communication—like predictive text or auto-generated responses—could lead to a streamlining of language, where shorthand terms or emojis become more common as a way to communicate quickly and efficiently. It's possible that we might see slang that simplifies or shortens common phrases, making communication faster and more accessible, especially in real-time conversations online.

Virtual Reality and the Metaverse

As virtual reality (VR) and the metaverse become more mainstream, we are likely to see the emergence of slang tailored to these new, immersive environments. In these virtual spaces, communication is not limited to text or voice alone; it involves gestures, avatars, and other forms of interaction. This opens up entirely new ways to express ideas, emotions, and identities, and it will undoubtedly give rise to slang that reflects these experiences.

In VR and metaverse spaces, users often communicate with avatars or virtual personas, where non-verbal cues—such as movement, expressions, and even body language—become just as important as words. This could lead to the creation of slang that's not only based on language but also on visual or physical cues. For example, the way someone "moves" in VR might be described with a term that could quickly become shorthand for a specific type of action or interaction. Words like "glitching" or "ghosting" might take on new meanings within the context of VR, with users adopting these terms to describe particular avatars' behavior or virtual phenomena.

The unique culture and behavior that emerge in the metaverse could shape entirely new slang terms that capture the digital life experience. Just as slang on TikTok and Instagram reflects online trends, the metaverse will likely cultivate a new vocabulary that speaks to the immersive and often surreal nature of virtual worlds. Terms related to navigating these spaces, engaging with digital objects, or even interacting with artificial intelligence characters could evolve quickly, creating an entirely new subculture of language.

New Communication Platforms and Their Impact on Slang

The rise of communication platforms like Discord, Clubhouse, and other niche networks will continue to influence how slang develops in the future. These platforms, many of which focus on real-time conversation and community engagement, are already cultivating unique dialects and slang among their user bases.

For instance, Discord has fostered an entire language of its own, where terms like "fomo" (fear of missing out), "pings" (notifications), and "squad" (group of friends) have taken on new life within its environment. The platform's emphasis on community and shared interest groups leads to slang that's specific to certain subcultures—whether those are gaming communities, tech enthusiasts, or music lovers. As these platforms grow, they will continue to drive the creation of slang that is niche but often crosses over into mainstream use.

Similarly, Clubhouse, which is centered around audio-based social interaction, has popularized terms like "room," "stage," and "mic drop" in new contexts. As more platforms emerge, each with its own distinct format, communication style, and focus, we can expect new sets of slang to evolve that are specific to those platforms but will eventually spill over into broader conversations.

Moreover, the influence of these platforms on slang is enhanced by the speed at which trends can spread. Just as TikTok has made it easy for new phrases, dance moves, and challenges to go viral, platforms like Discord and Clubhouse allow slang to spread organically within niche communities before reaching a wider audience.

The Intersection of Technology and Language

Technology has not only changed the way we communicate but also the way language itself evolves. From the rise of emojis and GIFs to the development of AI-driven language models, technology is continuously shaping the vocabulary we use and the ways we interact with each other.

In the future, we might see an even greater fusion of text, visuals, and gestures—where slang becomes multimodal, incorporating not just words but images, sounds, and even interactive elements. With AI-generated slang and the influence of VR, the very definition of language may expand, moving beyond the constraints of traditional text-based communication to encompass new digital experiences and expressions.

Slang will continue to be a mirror of the times—reflecting societal shifts, technological advancements, and cultural movements. And as new platforms and technologies emerge, so too will new ways of speaking, writing, and expressing ourselves. The role of technology in the future of slang is clear: it will continue to be an essential catalyst for the evolution of language, driving creativity, communication, and connection in exciting new directions.

The future of Gen Z slang is a reflection of how language evolves in response to the world around it. As new technologies and platforms continue to emerge, the way we communicate will change, and so will the words we use. From the rise of new social media platforms to the continued globalization of culture, the next wave of slang will likely be shaped by even faster, more diverse, and more interactive forms of communication. As we look ahead, it's clear that Gen Z's impact on language is just the beginning of a broader transformation in how we connect, relate, and express ourselves in the digital age. Understanding these shifts today will help us stay connected with the future of language tomorrow.

Chapter 6

Understanding the Cultural Significance of Slang

Slang is more than just a set of words or phrases; it's a living, breathing reflection of the culture that creates and adopts it. It encapsulates the mood, identity, and values of a generation, often emerging as a way to define one's unique social group and distinguish it from others. For Gen Z, slang has become a cornerstone of their cultural identity, a language that connects them to their peers and signals both rebellion and creativity. This chapter will explore the deeper cultural significance of Gen Z slang, examining how it functions as a tool for identity formation, social cohesion, and resistance, as well as its role in shaping societal narratives. Understanding the cultural context behind slang allows us to not only appreciate its power but also to engage with it in meaningful ways.

Slang as Cultural Expression

Language has always been a powerful tool for cultural expression. For Gen Z, slang is not just a way to communicate—it's a reflection of their values, attitudes, and the broader social issues they care about. Slang serves as both a mirror and a mold, shaping how this generation sees itself and how it wants to be seen by others. The way Gen Z speaks is directly tied to their quest for authenticity, individuality, and connection in an increasingly digital world.

Take the phrase "No cap" for example. Originally derived from hip-hop culture, "cap" refers to lying, and "no cap" means "no lie" or "I'm telling the truth." This phrase underscores Gen Z's desire for honesty and transparency. They reject the polished, curated facades often presented on social media, instead valuing raw, unfiltered conversations. In a world where authenticity is prized above all, "no cap" has become a shorthand for genuine, no-strings-attached communication. It's not just a catchphrase—it's a call to be real.

Similarly, the term "Bet" has grown popular as a simple expression of agreement or affirmation. It's an efficient, confident response, encapsulating Gen Z's emphasis on quick, direct interactions. "Bet" is a powerful, almost defiant term that showcases how this generation values autonomy and decisiveness. It's not a word that lingers or leaves room for ambiguity—it's clear, final, and empowering. It's a linguistic microcosm of a generation that has grown up with rapid information and fast-paced decision-making.

These terms, and many others, also hint at a subtle rebellion against the norms of the past. In some ways, slang functions as a form of cultural resistance—an act of defiance against older generations' expectations and a way to reclaim language from its historical roots. For Gen Z, every word they use has meaning, and they often choose their terms carefully, not only to communicate but to express their core beliefs about society and how they fit into it.

Through slang, Gen Z articulates their worldview—one where realness matters more than perfection, and where social connection is fast, flexible, and ever-evolving. Each new term they adopt is a reflection of their unique experiences in a world that's constantly shifting under their feet. And as slang continues to evolve, so too will the values and issues that shape it, ensuring that the language of tomorrow will continue to reflect the cultural pulse of Gen Z.

Slang and Identity

Language has always been a powerful tool for building identity and establishing connections, and for Gen Z, slang plays a crucial role in defining who they are—both as individuals and as a collective group. In many ways, slang acts as a badge of membership, signaling belonging to specific communities, subcultures, or even digital tribes. It serves as a social glue, binding people together through shared vocabulary, inside jokes, and cultural references.

For Gen Z, the use of slang is deeply tied to the creation of social boundaries. These boundaries are not just defined by geography or age, but by shared experiences, values, and even attitudes toward technology. When a group adopts a particular term or phrase, it becomes an implicit marker of membership. Using the right words at the right time can signal to others that you understand the cultural codes of a group, creating an instant bond and a sense of belonging. Take, for instance, the term "Vibe". In its most simple form, it's a descriptor of the mood or energy of a situation. But in the hands of Gen Z, it's much more—it's an expression of how they view and connect with the world around them. If you say "I'm vibing," it's not just about a mood; it's about aligning yourself with a group that values personal freedom, emotional authenticity, and social connection.

This connection through language is further amplified in online spaces. On platforms like TikTok, Discord, and Instagram, slang has become a crucial means of defining in-group vs. out-group dynamics. Terms like "Bet" or "Cap" are not just linguistic tools—they are markers of digital inclusion. The use of these words signals that you are part of the cultural moment, that you understand the references, and that you can participate in the ongoing social conversation. Slang, in this sense, fosters a sense of unity within these digital communities, allowing people to form friendships, networks, and shared identities across borders and backgrounds.

But beyond just creating bonds, slang also serves to reinforce social boundaries and distinctions. For Gen Z, language is a way to define who is "in" and who is "out." The right slang can elevate someone into a particular cultural group, while the wrong usage—or using outdated or "cringe" terms—can result in exclusion or ridicule. This phenomenon isn't new; language has always played a role in creating group identity. What's different now is the speed and reach at which slang spreads, thanks to the internet and social media platforms. A phrase that begins in one corner of the internet can quickly become part of global conversations, with the potential to unite or divide people based on their ability to understand and use it correctly.

Ultimately, Gen Z's use of slang is more than just a way to communicate—it's a means of crafting and defining identity. Through their language, they express who they are, who they stand with, and who they stand apart from. And as language continues to evolve, so too will the communities and identities that form around it, ensuring that slang remains a powerful tool for social connection and distinction.

The Global Spread of Slang

What began as a regional or even subcultural phenomenon has evolved into a global linguistic movement, and Gen Z slang is no exception. Thanks to the power of social media, platforms like TikTok, Twitter, and Instagram have acted as accelerators for the rapid spread of language, making it possible for Gen Z slang to transcend geographic, cultural, and linguistic boundaries. What was once specific to certain neighborhoods, cities, or countries is now being adopted, adapted, and remixed worldwide. This unprecedented global exchange of language has created a shared, interconnected lexicon that stretches far beyond the borders of the United States.

Social media has been the great equalizer, uniting people from different parts of the world with a common language—one that is malleable, ever-changing, and highly influenced by memes, trends, and viral content. The universal appeal of platforms like TikTok has helped propel Gen Z slang into the global spotlight, where it's been picked up by users from diverse countries and cultures. For example, terms like "Bet", "No Cap", or "Vibe" are now widely recognized and understood not only by young people in America, but also by Gen Z in Europe, Asia, Latin America, and even parts of Africa.

But the influence of Gen Z slang isn't always one-way. While American slang terms have been quickly adopted abroad, they often undergo regional transformation. What starts as a shared term can evolve to take on new meanings, depending on local cultures, languages, or contexts. Consider how the term "Flex"—which originally means to show off—has taken on slightly different meanings depending on the country or community. In some areas, it still refers to boasting, while in others, it's used more ironically, to imply that someone is overcompensating or even trying too hard.

This is a phenomenon that's particularly noticeable in the way memes and viral phrases cross borders and adapt. For instance, a phrase like "Cheugy", which originally emerged in the U.S. to describe outdated or uncool trends, has become a global sensation, albeit with regional variations. In the UK, for instance, "Cheugy" has expanded to describe certain fashion trends, like wearing low-rise jeans or oversized logos, that are seen as passé or cringe. Similarly, "Mood", which in the U.S. often serves as an empathetic expression of agreement ("Same here"), is sometimes used in other countries with slight shifts in meaning or context, depending on the cultural nuances of how it is adopted.

Another fascinating example of the global spread of Gen Z slang is "Sis", a term of endearment that began as part of African American Vernacular English (AAVE) but has since found its way into the lexicon of Gen Z across the world. Whether used in the U.S., the UK, or Australia, the term is now widely used to refer to a close friend or to show camaraderie, though its tone and significance can shift depending on the relationship between the speaker and the listener. In Brazil, "Sis" has taken on a slightly more playful, often sarcastic tone, reflecting the playful and warm-hearted nature of Brazilian youth culture.

The global nature of Gen Z slang is also evident in how memes and phrases take on unique forms in different regions. A perfect example of this is the "OK Boomer" meme. Initially used to mock older generations in the U.S., the phrase quickly became a worldwide expression, with variations in how it's deployed. In countries like New Zealand and Australia, the meme spread like wildfire but took on a broader generational connotation, addressing not just Baby Boomers but anyone seen as out of touch with youth culture. The phrase became a sort of universal symbol of generational conflict, sparking a global conversation that resonated with young people worldwide.

This phenomenon is indicative of a larger trend in language evolution: the internet is creating a shared linguistic space that transcends borders, and Gen Z slang has emerged as a powerful tool for expressing youth culture and rebellion in a global context. As language and culture continue to intertwine across platforms, slang terms are no longer bound by geography. Instead, they have become part of a broader, interconnected global conversation that shapes how Gen Z communicates, identifies, and connects with one another.

In this way, Gen Z slang is a true reflection of a more globalized, digital world. It not only connects young people from different corners of the earth, but it also reflects the shifting cultural values that transcend nations. The fluidity of language, the rapid sharing of trends, and the adaptability of slang have made it a global phenomenon—a phenomenon that shows no signs of slowing down. As long as social media continues to thrive, the global spread of Gen Z slang will only intensify, with new phrases, memes, and words constantly being born, evolving, and circulating on a scale never before seen in human history.

Slang is a mirror of the times, constantly adapting and evolving in response to the cultural and social climates from which it arises. For Gen Z, it serves not only as a way to communicate but also as a form of self-expression, a rebellion against the conventional, and a marker of their distinct worldview. By understanding the cultural significance behind the slang, we gain a richer appreciation for the forces that drive language and the social movements it reflects. As we look to the future, it's clear that slang will continue to play a pivotal role in shaping identities, creating communities, and reflecting the ever-changing tides of culture. Slang is not just a linguistic trend; it's a cultural phenomenon.

Chapter 7

Building Stronger Relationships Through Language

Language is more than just a means of communication—it's the bridge that connects us to others. In today's world, where digital interactions dominate, the ability to connect through shared language has never been more important. Gen Z slang, with its humor, authenticity, and creativity, serves as a unique tool for strengthening relationships, especially between different generations. By understanding and incorporating Gen Z slang, individuals can enhance their ability to engage, build trust, and establish genuine connections. This chapter explores how language—specifically Gen Z slang—can be a powerful tool for building stronger relationships, whether with friends, family, colleagues, or even strangers.

Communication Across Generations

In today's rapidly evolving world, generational divides in communication styles are more apparent than ever. Gen

Z, the youngest generation, has grown up in a digital-first world, where the way they communicate is vastly different from older generations. While Baby Boomers and Gen X might favor face-to-face conversations or long-form communication, Gen Z has embraced short, quick exchanges—often with a heavy reliance on slang, memes, and digital shorthand. Understanding this new linguistic landscape is crucial, not only for staying relevant but for bridging the gap between generations.

When older generations make the effort to understand and use Gen Z slang, it serves as a gesture of respect and willingness to connect. Using the same language doesn't just create a common ground; it also helps foster better conversations by demonstrating that we're open to understanding the nuances of the younger generation. For instance, when an older manager uses terms like "bet" or "slay" in the office, it's not about mimicking youth culture, but about showing that they're paying attention to the language Gen Z uses. This small effort can break down barriers, signaling openness and adaptability.

Slang, when used authentically, has the potential to level the playing field between generations, creating a shared space where everyone feels heard and understood. It's not just about the words themselves but what they represent—the values, attitudes, and lived experiences of those who use them. For example, terms like "no cap" or "lowkey" convey a sense of honesty, transparency, and subtlety that Gen Z cherishes. When older generations acknowledge these values by using the slang appropriately, it fosters mutual respect and encourages more fluid, natural communication. Rather than feeling alienated by the new language, people from different generations can feel included, creating a collaborative environment where ideas flow freely.

In essence, using and understanding Gen Z slang isn't about trying to "fit in" with the younger generation, but about fostering communication that's both inclusive and meaningful. By making the effort to bridge the gap, individuals from all generations can create stronger, more empathetic connections, helping to build a culture of respect, understanding, and cooperation in both personal and professional spaces.

The Role of Slang in Strengthening Personal Relationships

Language has always been a powerful tool in building connections. The words we choose and the way we communicate shape how we relate to others. For Gen Z, slang has become not just a linguistic trend but a bond that ties them together. It's how they express individuality, align with their peers, and communicate authenticity. For older generations, tapping into this evolving language can be an incredibly effective way to build rapport, break down generational barriers, and make interactions feel more genuine and connected.

When you use Gen Z slang in your conversations, especially with younger people, it signals that you're attuned to their world. It shows that you're not only willing to embrace their way of communicating, but that you understand and respect it. Whether you're talking to a younger sibling, a colleague, or even your children, using slang can make your interactions feel less formal and more comfortable. For instance, saying "That was lit!" in response to an exciting story from a younger family member or "I'm vibing" after a shared experience can immediately create a sense of shared excitement. These small but significant gestures let them know that you're "in the know" and part of their social world.

More than just the words themselves, using slang shows that you're engaged in the conversation. It's a sign that you care enough to speak the same language as the other person, without trying to sound inauthentic. Imagine texting your teen: instead of saying, "That sounds like a fun idea," you say, "Bet, I'm in!" The conversation feels lighter, more casual, and more in tune with how Gen Z communicates. In these moments, the relationship moves beyond a hierarchical exchange and becomes more of a partnership, where both sides are speaking on equal terms.

Moreover, slang allows for a shared sense of humor and inside jokes. When you adopt terms like "slay" or "sus," you're not just using language, you're becoming part of the cultural tapestry that these phrases represent. These small linguistic shifts bring an emotional depth to interactions, helping younger individuals feel heard, valued, and understood. It's no longer about just being an authority figure or an older person trying to relate. It's about becoming a peer in a way that's accessible, respectful, and authentic.

At work, using Gen Z slang can also humanize your relationships with younger colleagues. When a manager or supervisor uses terms like "Bet" or "No cap" in meetings, it shows they're approachable and relatable, removing the sense of distance that sometimes exists between different generations in the workplace. This can encourage open dialogue and make the work environment feel more inclusive. Imagine a boss who says, "That was lit!" when praising a team achievement, or "No cap, this project is going to be huge." These phrases can inspire a sense of excitement and camaraderie that might not otherwise be there, making team interactions feel more human and less corporate.

In personal relationships, too, slang can deepen bonds. For instance, when you use slang with friends or family members, it's a way of speaking a shared "language" that instantly connects you. If your teenage niece says, "This TikTok is fire!" and you respond with, "Yeah, that was totally slay," you're not only acknowledging their interests but also speaking their emotional language. This doesn't mean you have to overdo it or use every new term that pops up, but rather, it's about making those little, meaningful connections. They appreciate that you're in tune with their world, and in return, you create an emotional resonance that can deepen your relationship.

In conclusion, using Gen Z slang to strengthen personal relationships is not about adopting every term you hear or trying to mimic youth culture. It's about speaking in a way that resonates with the younger generation—showing empathy, understanding, and connection through shared language. When you embrace this evolving linguistic landscape, you're not just bridging generational gaps; you're building meaningful, personal connections that are both genuine and lasting. Whether in family gatherings, friendships, or the workplace, using slang appropriately fosters an environment of mutual respect and open communication—making every interaction feel more relatable, more personal, and more authentic.

When to Use Slang and When to Be Formal

Language is a dynamic and powerful tool, and the context in which you use it can determine the success of your communication. Gen Z slang, while a fun and engaging way to connect with younger individuals, isn't always appropriate for every situation. Knowing when to use slang and when to adopt a more formal tone is essential for ensuring you're understood and respected across different environments.

Situations Where Slang is Appropriate

1. Informal Conversations with Friends and Family:
Slang thrives in casual, relaxed settings where the primary goal is connection and camaraderie. Conversations with friends, siblings, or younger relatives are prime opportunities to use slang. In these settings, using terms like "lit," "bet," or "vibe" can make interactions feel lighter and more relatable, helping you bond over shared experiences. For example, texting a friend, "That movie was fire!" is a great way to convey excitement without the stiffness of formal language.

2. Social Media and Online Interactions:
Platforms like TikTok, Instagram, and Twitter are hubs where slang reigns supreme. Using slang in comments,

captions, or direct messages aligns you with the culture of these platforms and signals that you're in tune with the current social discourse. This is especially true when engaging with younger users. The fluid, informal nature of online communication means that using terms like "no cap" or "slay" can help you fit in and keep the conversation engaging.

3. Team or Peer-Based Settings:

In collaborative environments like school group projects, creative brainstorms, or casual work meetings, slang can help break down barriers and foster teamwork. A casual "That idea is fire" or "Bet, let's do it!" can energize the group and create a more relaxed atmosphere. It shows that you're approachable and part of the team, reducing the formality of group dynamics and encouraging more open participation.

Situations Where Formal Language is More Appropriate

1. Professional or Business Settings:

In the workplace or during business communications, the use of slang should be minimal and carefully considered. While some slang can help build rapport with younger colleagues or clients, overusing it in formal emails, meetings, or presentations could come across as unprofessional. Terms like "slay" or "bet" might feel out of place in a corporate strategy session or when discussing serious matters. Instead, it's better to rely on clear, concise language that conveys your ideas without ambiguity. When in doubt, choose formality over slang.

2. *Public Speaking or Academic Contexts:*

Whether you're presenting at a conference, teaching a class, or delivering a speech, formal language should dominate. Slang may undermine your authority or detract from the seriousness of your message. Using terms like "sus" or "vibing" might alienate your audience, especially in settings where clarity and professionalism are key. When addressing a broad audience, especially those outside your immediate social circle, it's important to use language that is universally understood and doesn't rely on in-group vernacular.

3. *Written Communication in Professional or Legal Contexts:*

In formal emails, reports, legal documents, and official letters, sticking to proper grammar and formal language is essential. Slang can be misinterpreted, especially in written form where tone is harder to convey. While informal communication, like texting or chatting online, may allow slang, written professional exchanges should be clear and direct, leaving little room for misunderstanding. For example, instead of writing "No cap, the project's deadline is tight," a more appropriate phrasing would be, "The project deadline is quickly approaching and requires immediate attention."

Striking the Right Balance

Understanding the balance between casual and formal language is key to effective communication. In social settings, slang can enhance relationships and signal that you're part of a shared social group. However, in professional or public settings, it's important to switch to a more formal register to ensure clarity and respect for the audience or situation. Knowing the distinction is crucial for avoiding awkward or inappropriate moments where your language could unintentionally undermine your message or make you seem out of touch.

One way to strike the right balance is to read the room and assess your audience. If you're in a more relaxed setting, using slang can feel natural and engaging. But if you're in a professional meeting or talking to someone in a more formal context, it's best to err on the side of caution and choose a language that feels appropriate for the situation.

In summary, knowing when to use slang and when to be formal is a key skill in today's communication landscape. Slang can help you build stronger personal connections, especially with younger people, but using it indiscriminately in formal settings can backfire. By staying attuned to the social context and understanding the expectations of your audience, you can use slang effectively to create stronger, more authentic relationships, without compromising professionalism or respect.

As we navigate a world increasingly driven by digital communication, the importance of connecting through language cannot be overstated. Gen Z slang, with its dynamic nature and cultural relevance, offers a unique opportunity to bridge generational divides and foster authentic relationships. By using slang with understanding and empathy, we can create a shared space where communication flows more naturally, and mutual respect thrives. Whether in personal interactions or professional settings, embracing this evolving language helps us stay relevant, relatable, and engaged with one another. Understanding and using Gen Z slang is not just about speaking their language; it's about speaking their truth, building trust, and fostering deeper connections in a rapidly changing world.

Conclusion

The world of language is a living, breathing entity that continually evolves. Slang, particularly Gen Z slang, is not just a collection of trendy phrases—it's a reflection of the values, attitudes, and experiences of an entire generation. It's a lens through which we can better understand the world in which we live, and an essential tool for staying connected to the cultural pulse of today's youth. Throughout this book, we've explored the importance of understanding Gen Z slang, how to use it effectively, and how it plays a crucial role in shaping communication, relationships, and even social movements.

Recap of Key Points

At the core of Gen Z slang is the desire for authenticity and connection. From the introduction of terms like "cap" and "no cap" to the cultural phenomena that shaped phrases like "slay" and "bet," we've witnessed how slang provides insight into a generation that values directness, inclusivity, and creativity. These words are not just used for fun; they serve as tools for expressing individuality, forming bonds, and navigating the complexities of modern social landscapes.

We've also delved into how slang is influenced by various factors, including social media, internet culture, and youth subcultures. Platforms like TikTok, Instagram, and Twitter have acted as accelerants, helping Gen Z slang spread and evolve at lightning speed. This digital-first generation has embraced these platforms not just as tools for entertainment, but as places where language can be shaped, shared, and redefined.

More importantly, we discussed how to use Gen Z slang effectively. It's not just about knowing the meanings of terms like "lit" or "vibe" — it's about understanding when and where to use them, ensuring you don't sound forced or inauthentic. Slang can be a powerful bridge, connecting people across generations and cultural divides, but only when used appropriately. Whether in casual conversations with friends or in professional settings with colleagues, choosing the right words can enhance communication and strengthen relationships.

The book also highlighted some slang terms that have overstayed their welcome or have become cringeworthy, serving as a reminder that not all slang is meant to last. Language is fluid, and what's popular today can easily become outdated tomorrow. Recognizing when to let go of certain terms is just as important as knowing when to use new ones.

In the end, the journey through Gen Z slang serves as a testament to the dynamic nature of language itself. Just as previous generations saw their own unique slang come and go, Gen Z will eventually pass the baton to the next wave of linguistic innovators. Language will continue to adapt, shift, and reflect the cultural and technological changes that shape each generation.

Final Thoughts on Slang

Slang, as a form of language, is much more than just a collection of cool phrases. It represents the voices of a generation, echoing their desires, frustrations, and ambitions. In a world that is more connected than ever before, slang is the social glue that brings us closer together. It allows us to navigate the complex world of online and offline relationships, and it plays a central role in helping us forge new identities and communities.

As we've seen in this book, understanding and using slang isn't just for the young. It's a vital part of modern communication that transcends age, allowing for authentic expression and connection. Whether you're a teenager trying to keep up with the latest trends or an older professional trying to connect with younger colleagues, being attuned to the language of the moment is a key element of successful communication.

Gen Z's slang may seem like a fleeting trend, but in reality, it's part of a much larger, ongoing conversation about language, culture, and identity. The digital age, with its ever-expanding platforms, is the stage on which this conversation plays out. Social media, gaming, memes, and viral videos are the new frontiers where language is forged, and Gen Z is leading the charge. The slang they use today will likely influence the language of tomorrow, much like the slang of previous generations has shaped modern communication.

So, while it may seem overwhelming to keep up with the rapid pace of change, the key is to embrace the fluidity of language. Language, after all, is a reflection of society's evolution. By staying attuned to it, we can ensure that we remain connected, relevant, and engaged with the world around us.

Now that you've gained insight into the fascinating world of Gen Z slang, it's time to put what you've learned into practice. Don't just read about the terms—start using them! Be confident in experimenting with new slang, but remember to do so in a way that feels natural and true to your personality. It's not about forcing phrases into conversations, but rather about using language as a tool for connection, self-expression, and fun.

Whether you're engaging with friends, family, or colleagues, incorporating slang into your conversations can strengthen bonds and make interactions feel more genuine. Just remember to read the room—understanding the context and the audience is key to making sure your language is appropriate and effective. Use slang to create a sense of camaraderie, but also be mindful of when formal language might be more fitting.

Embrace the evolution of language, and as you do, take pride in being part of a larger cultural shift that's shaping the way we communicate. The next time you drop a "bet" or vibe with your friends, you'll be more than just speaking Gen Z slang—you'll be connecting with a powerful, evolving movement of language that transcends generations.

As you continue your journey, don't be afraid to ask questions, make mistakes, and most importantly, enjoy the ride. Language is meant to be playful, flexible, and ever-changing. So, go ahead—slay that conversation, no cap.

105

Appendices

Appendix A: Slang Cheat Sheet

This cheat sheet serves as a quick reference guide for the most popular and widely used Gen Z slang terms. Whether you're trying to brush up on your slang knowledge or just need a fast refresher, this list will help you understand and use these terms confidently. Keep it handy for your next conversation!

1. Cap / No Cap
- Definition: "Cap" means a lie, and "No cap" means no lie or telling the truth.
  Example:
- "You're capping!" (You're lying.)
- "No cap, I love that movie!" (I'm being honest, I really do like it.)

2. Bet
- Definition: An expression of agreement, confirmation, or affirmation.
  Example:
- Wanna hang out later?" "Bet!" (Yes, sounds good!)

3. Slay

- Definition: To do something exceptionally well, often with confidence and style.
  Example:
- "You slayed that presentation!" (You did an amazing job!)

4. Lit

- Definition: Used to describe something that's exciting, fun, or amazing.
  Example:
- "That concert was lit!" (That concert was incredible!)

5. Vibe / Vibing

- Definition: Describes the mood or feeling of a person, place, or situation.
  Example:
- "I'm just vibing right now." (I'm just chilling and enjoying the moment.)

6. Tea

- Definition: Gossip or the latest news.
  Example:
- "Spill the tea!" (Tell me the gossip!)

7. Stan

- Definition: To be a fan or supporter of something or someone intensely.
  Example:
- "I totally stan that band!" (I'm a huge fan of that band!)

8. Extra

- Definition: Over-the-top or excessive behavior.
  Example:
- "She's being so extra with that outfit!" (She's trying too hard with that outfit.)

9. Ghosting

- Definition: The act of abruptly stopping all communication without explanation.
  Example:
- "I thought we were getting along, but then he ghosted me." (He stopped talking to me without reason.)

10. FOMO

- Definition: Fear of missing out; anxiety over potentially missing an exciting event.

Example:

- "I'm getting major FOMO seeing everyone at that party!" (I'm feeling anxious that I missed out on the fun.)

11. Flex

- Definition: To show off or boast, often about material possessions or achievements.
  Example:
- "Stop flexing your new shoes!" (Stop showing off your new shoes.)

12. Fam

- Definition: Short for family, but often used to refer to close friends or your social circle.
  Example:
- "What's up, fam?" (Hey, friends!)

13. Sus

- Definition: Short for suspicious, used to describe something or someone that seems shady or untrustworthy.
  Example:
- "That's kind of sus." (That seems suspicious.)

14. Clout

- Definition: Influence, power, or social standing, often used to describe someone who is popular or well-known.
  Example:
- "She's just doing it for the clout." (She's doing it for attention or fame.)

15. No Cap

- Definition: No lie; used to emphasize truthfulness.
  Example:
- "No cap, that's the best burger I've ever had!" (I'm serious, it's the best!)

16. Lowkey / Highkey

- Definition: "Lowkey" means something subtle or not obvious, while "Highkey" is the opposite, meaning something very obvious or loud.
  Example:
- "I lowkey want to stay home today." (I kind of want to stay home but I'm not saying it out loud.)
- "I highkey love that song!" (I absolutely love that song!)

17. LMAO

- Definition: An acronym for "Laughing My Ass Off," used to indicate something is very funny.
  Example:
- "That joke had me LMAO!" (That joke made me laugh a lot!)

18. Vibing

- Definition: To be in sync with a situation or to enjoy a moment.
  Example:
- "I'm just vibing with my friends at the beach." (We're having a great time together.)

19. Savage

- Definition: Bold, fearless, or ruthless. Often used to describe someone who is unapologetically confident.
  Example:
- "That comeback was savage!" (That response was bold and impressive.)

20. Shook

- Definition: Shocked, surprised, or overwhelmed by something.
  Example:
- "I was shook when I saw that plot twist!" (I was really surprised by that plot twist.)

Appendix B: Resources for Learning More

Gen Z slang is constantly evolving, and staying up-to-date with the latest terms can be tricky. Fortunately, there are a variety of online resources and social media platforms that can help you keep your slang game strong. Here are some go-to places for staying in the loop:

1. TikTok

- Why: TikTok is the breeding ground for new slang. Trends and viral challenges often introduce new words and phrases, which spread rapidly across social media platforms.
- How to use it: Follow creators who regularly use Gen Z slang in their videos, or search for hashtags like #GenZSlang or #Slang.

2. X (Twitter)

- Why: Twitter is a hotbed for discussions around the latest trends, including slang. Many words and phrases start trending here before they hit other platforms.
- How to use it: Keep an eye on trending hashtags, especially those related to youth culture or current events, to discover new slang.

3. Instagram

- Why: Instagram is not just a photo-sharing platform; it's where memes and other cultural trends often spread. Gen Z slang is frequently featured in memes, stories, and captions.
- How to use it: Follow meme accounts or youth culture influencers to stay up-to-date with the latest slang.

4. Urban Dictionary

- Why: Urban Dictionary is one of the most comprehensive online resources for slang definitions, including Gen Z-specific terms.
- How to use it: Search for new slang terms as they emerge to get the most accurate and up-to-date meanings.

5. Reddit

- Why: Subreddits like r/OutOfTheLoop and r/GenZ are great places to explore new slang. Users discuss and break down language trends regularly.
- How to use it: Engage in discussions about trends or ask for explanations of slang you encounter.

6. YouTube

- Why: Many YouTube channels explain and dissect Gen Z slang in fun, educational ways.
- How to use it: Look for videos titled "Gen Z Slang Explained" or "How to Speak Like Gen Z" for breakdowns and tutorials.

7. Memes and Social Media Pages

- Why: Websites and Instagram accounts dedicated to memes often feature the most recent Gen Z terms.
- How to use it: Follow meme pages or check websites like Meme Generator, Know Your Meme, or Memedroid.

8. Slang Dictionary Apps

- Why: Various apps dedicated to slang (e.g., Slang Dictionary or Urban Slang Dictionary) provide easy access to definitions and examples on the go.
- How to use it: Download one of these apps to quickly check any term you encounter in real-time conversations.

By leveraging these resources, you can continue to stay connected with the ever-evolving world of Gen Z slang, ensuring you never miss out on the next big trend.

About the Author

Janet E. Shaw is a passionate linguist, writer, and cultural observer with a deep interest in the evolving landscape of language, especially among younger generations. With a background in communication and cultural studies, Janet has spent years studying the intersection of technology, youth culture, and language, focusing on how digital platforms and social media are reshaping the way we speak, connect, and understand one another.

Throughout her career, Janet has worked as a writer, editor, and educator, with a particular focus on bridging generational gaps through language. She is fascinated by the ways in which language reflects the values and experiences of a generation, and how slang serves as both a tool for self-expression and a marker of identity. Her academic research has been published in various journals, and her insights into Gen Z culture have made her a sought-after speaker and consultant on topics of youth communication, digital culture, and language trends.

In addition to her professional work, Janet is an avid consumer of digital media, spending time on platforms like TikTok, Twitter, and Instagram to stay connected with the pulse of contemporary youth language. She believes that language is not just a tool for communication, but a dynamic force that continuously shapes and defines the cultural landscape.

When she's not writing or researching, Janet enjoys traveling, exploring new cultures, and teaching young people how to harness the power of language to express their ideas and connect with others in meaningful ways. This book is the culmination of her years of study and personal fascination with the world of Gen Z slang, offering readers a unique lens through which to better understand the rapidly changing language of today's youth.